Student
DARES

GW00722377

summersdale

STUDENT DARES

Copyright © Summersdale Publishers Ltd, 2005

Reprinted 2006 and 2007

Text by Steph Little

Summersdale Publishers Ltd
46 West Street
Chichester
West Sussex
PO19 1RP
UK

www.summersdale.com

Printed and bound in Great Britain

ISBN: 1-84024-451-8
ISBN 13: 978-1-84024-451-9

About the Author

Steph Little attended school, college and university, and left a trail of destruction and confusion in her wake. She is also the author of *Office Dares*.

*For everyone in Lambert Hall B,
The Lawns, 2001*

Contents

Introduction

For at least twelve years of our early lives, we are forced to attend school. Some people go on to higher education, and even university. But the fact of the matter is: education is boring, learning is dull. The education system is sapping the fun from millions of students across the nation. Who's to say we can't inject a little entertainment into our classrooms?

There are dares in this book to be played in the classroom, the library, in halls of residence and during extracurricular activities. Feel free to mix it up and make things more interesting.

Remember, we are all in this together. It is up to each and every one of us to rise to the challenge and make learning institutions across the land a little bit more tolerable. It is time to embrace your inner delinquent.

Student
DARES

WARNING NO. 1: Playing Student Dares will not reward you with the grades you have always dreamt of, but rest assured you will leave the classroom safe in the knowledge that you have brightened up the day of every student. Or just confused the hell out of them.

WARNING NO. 2: Use this book wisely. Amuse and perplex your tutors, but don't make them cry. They are the ones who mark your papers, and they will remember you at your graduation.

A quick note about the point system:

The dares have been given a carefully graded point system. Warm yourself up with the 1 point dares: they are perfect for the confident beginner or for your first day in a new group.

The 3 point dares are easy to perform but are sometimes so subtle they may go unnoticed.

The 5 point dares are not to be taken lightly. They are challenging and somewhat outrageous. Expect very puzzled glances and to lose friends.

If it is your last day at college or you are sure expulsion is looming on the horizon, by all means turn straight to the 10 point dares. Do not blame me for the consequences.

Play the game, if you dare…

In the classroom...

From primary school through to university, the classroom remains the educational and social hub of the academic world. The perfect place to unleash your daring side…

1 point dares

Whenever the group is called upon to answer a question, volunteer yourself, answer incorrectly and then shoot your tutor with double-barrelled fingers.

Arrive 20 minutes early for a lesson and stand to attention outside the door. If anyone questions you, simply reply (in character), 'There are no questions allowed in Communist Russia.'

During a history discussion stand up and inquire, 'Is there nothing new in this lesson?'

After every sentence add the word 'innit': 'Darwin argued that evolution was controlled by forces of natural selection... innit.'

18

Keep a fork in your pencil case.
When your lecturer asks you
to do something, look at them
through the prongs, and imagine
them serving time.

See how many times you can get away with going to the toilet during one lesson. Blame it on a heavy night's drinking.

At the end of class, shake your tutor's hand and congratulate them on an excellent lesson.

When responding to a question, raise two hands instead of one.

3 point dares

When your name is called in a register, say 'I will answer this time, but in future please refer to me as Fabio.'

When overcome by boredom in an English seminar, mutter famous lines from Shakespearean plays under your breath until your teacher notices. If disturbed, reply with a dramatic rendition of Mercutio's death… 'A plague on both your houses!'

24

When your tutor mentions a number, call out 'Bingo!' Apologise and explain that you got confused.

Roll your eyes and shake your head in disagreement each time your tutor speaks.

Student DARES

If someone comes into the lecture theatre, gasp as they enter and sigh as they leave.

Stay behind after class and ask the cleaners if they wouldn't mind giving you a quick once over.

Fashion a paper banner that reads 'You're a genius' and unroll it at the end of a lecture, as a gesture of appreciation for the guest speaker.

29

At the start of a class place your chair at the tutor's desk and ask for some one-to-one tuition.

Hand in an essay to your art tutor on why Michelangelo got to be one of the Turtles but Van Gogh didn't.

5 point dares

Leave whatever lesson you are in at 11.30 on the dot, proclaiming it is time for a Diet Coke break.

Stand up and demand to know the real reason you are all together in the classroom.

Refer to your teacher as 'Chief' every time you speak to them.

Midway through a lesson pull out a packed lunch and begin eating. When your actions are questioned, ask, 'Don't we get a break?' Offer your teacher a crisp.

At the end of the lesson, hug your tutor and request to see 'more of the same' next time.

Dispute everything your tutor says, no matter how simple. Whenever your tutor makes a statement, ask them, 'Can you prove it?'

Arrive early for a class. Give yourself enough time to rearrange all of the tables into a makeshift fort, of which you are king.

During class, slowly edge your
chair towards the door.

10 point dares

Arrange for a clown to come and perform during a Theology seminar.

Carve a bust of your tutor out of cheese. Tie a ribbon round it and present it to them at the beginning of the class. Demand extra credit.

During a French class, stand up
and before storming out yell,
'This is NOT Lebanese.'

Knock on the faculty lounge door and ask if anyone is up for a pint after class.

43

Throw a surprise party for your tutor. Insist that you can't start the class until they have had a piece of cake. Ask a fellow student when the strippers are due to arrive.

Instead of taking notes, draw an abstract sketch of your tutor, entitled 'Professor Hot Lips'. Leave it on their desk as you leave.

Place a tape player inside your bag playing a loop of 'Hello? ... I am stuck in here... I'm frightened... Hello?'

Scores

There were a total of 145 points up for grabs in this section.

If you scored 0–50 points: You call yourself daring? You need to raise your game.

If you scored 51–100 points: A good effort. Now move on to the library dares: they will really test your skill.

If you scored 101+ points: That's the spirit! Keep up the excellent work.

In the library...

The library. A place of quiet study and calm repose. Or, depending on how you look at it, the Student Dare Land of Opportunity...

1 point dares

Go up to the front desk and ask where you might find the books.

Skip rather than walk.

Carry a pile of books so huge it completely obscures your view. Award yourself an extra point for each person you bump into.

Pull up a chair next to a stranger, get as close as you can and stare at their open book. When they look at you, bemused, say, 'So, what are we reading?'

Settle down to read a book.
Every time you turn a page,
emit a loud groan.

When checking out books at the desk, hand over your Tesco Clubcard. Request reward points.

3 point dares

Eyeball someone through the gap in the shelves. When they move, you move.

Shout 'Bollocks!' as loud
as you can. (Childish? Yes.
Funny? Oh yes.)

Organise a bunch of people
in the library to emit a low
humming noise while
keeping straight faces.

57

If a member of staff passes with a trolley of books, offer to push it for them. Wheel it in the opposite direction to which they were going.

Take your chair into the lift and visit all the floors, until you are asked to leave.

Move to the quietest area of the library. Shush everyone at regular intervals.

Whisper to someone,
'Can you hear that?'
'What?'
'Oh, nothing.'
Repeat five times.

5 point dares

Ask a member of staff to help you find a book you have had trouble locating. Ensure the book is in your hands, in full view.

62

Build a tower of books taller than yourself. Play Jenga™.

Walk around the library slowly
and try to push the bookshelves.
Pull on books as if they are
levers. Tell people you are
looking for the
secret passageway.

Set off the sensors at the door, and drop to the floor crying, 'I knew you would find me eventually.'

Approach the student who seems most engrossed in their book. Say, 'I am afraid I am going to have to ask you to leave.' If they ask why, simply reply, 'You know the rules.'

10 point dares

Take all the books off the bottom shelf of a secluded area. Climb in and lie down; stay perfectly still. Wait for someone to browse nearby, then yawn, slowly roll out from your makeshift napping space, stand up and walk away.

67

Move around the shelves as
if you are trapped inside a
computer game. Stealth along
the walls, cock your fake gun
and include suitably elaborate
sound effects.

Run a lap of the library at high speed. Look at your watch and announce a personal best. Repeat until physically restrained.

Scores

There were a total of 82 points up for grabs in this section.

If you scored 0–20 points: Are you even trying?

If you scored 21–50 points: You're really getting the hang of this now. And you're starting to love it, aren't you?

If you scored 51+ points: Excellent work. Have you noticed your tutor's worry lines getting deeper?

In the halls of residence...

Moving into halls of residence at university is often the first time we have lived away from home. The following dares provide the perfect opportunity to make friends or enemies for life...

71

1 point dares

Ignore the first five people who say hello to you.

Introduce yourself as Helmut/ Helga. Keep this up for a week.

When unpacking your belongings
in a shared bedroom, ask your
roommate, 'So, where can I keep
my snake?'

Cooking a meal for your hall-mates is a perfect way to make friends. Prepare turnip soup for starter, a liver stew for the main course and for dessert, a trifle made with fish.

75

Create a fake spider out of pipe cleaners. Hide it behind the butter in the fridge.

Walk up to people and ask them, very seriously, 'Do you know the muffin man?'

When cooking, stick a piece
of broccoli between your front
teeth. Smile a lot.

Announce when you are going to the bathroom. Be sure to specify which number it will be.

79

Leave your underpants hanging
in the shower.

3 point dares

Leave your zipper open.
If anyone points it out, say,
'I prefer it this way.'

Ask your hall-mates mysterious
questions then scribble furiously
in a notebook. Mutter something
about 'psychological profiles'.

From your window drop water bombs on passers-by. When bored of this, replace water with yoghurt.

Go into the room of a hall-
mate the night before an
important deadline, and while
they watch you with growing
irritation, turn the light switch
on and off ten times.

84

Drop a Snickers™ bar into the communal toilet. Leave a note on the door asking everyone to be more considerate when using the bathroom.

Tell everyone you meet that your father is David Hasselhoff.

Five days in advance, tell your new friends you cannot attend their party because you are not in the mood.

Put a huge bowl of jelly right outside someone's door...

... Fill the same person's shoes with more jelly, just in case they missed it the first time.

5 point dares

Sneak a pair of red pants into the washing machine. When a hall-mate's white clothes are found to be pink, blame it on the quiet bloke downstairs.

89

Convince people you are hard of hearing. Communicate in an incomprehensible sign language of your own warped invention.

Flirt with your room-mate's partner *really* badly. Lick your lips when they are talking to you and wink when they leave.

Get drunk, and accuse all members of the opposite sex of fancying you. In the morning, deny all knowledge.

Get drunk, and accuse someone of eating your cheese. Break into elaborate sobs and say you are moving out. In the morning, deny all knowledge.

Perform a morning ritual
of 'underwear yoga' in a
communal room.

Fashion a holster belt for the
remote control and wear
it with pride.

Bake a chocolate cake for everyone and lace it with chilli powder. Enjoy watching them pretend it is delicious.

Student
DARES

10 point dares
(best performed drunk)

Knock on the hall warden's door
at 3 a.m. and invite yourself in
for a nightcap.

Ask the least attractive bartender in the union bar if they will go out to dinner with you. If turned down, cry into your beer and explain that you are having such a difficult time fitting in at university. Repeat every night for a week.

Stand beneath someone's window and perform the Chesney classic, 'The One and Only'.

Scores

There were a total of 103 points up for grabs in this section.

If you scored 0–40 points: You are a loser. Give this book to someone with balls.

If you scored 41–80 points: Good work. Give yourself a pat on the back.

If you scored 81+ points: You are a shining example of daring behaviour. Bravo!

Extracurricular...

Whether you are captain of the football team or a member of the chess club, there will be a ludicrous dare for you to undertake in this section.

1 point dares

Join the chess club, then run out of the first meeting laughing and yelling, 'Nerds!'

Turn up to trampolining club
wearing a crash helmet.

Go to swimming club wearing arm bands. If asked to remove them, sob like a baby and ask for your mummy.

Arrive at the football tryouts
in full rugby kit. Tackle your
teammates rugby-style.

105

Join the film society. At the first meeting ask when *The Terminator* will be screened.

Attend badminton training.
Whenever the coach says the
word 'shuttlecock' giggle like
a little girl.

3 point dares

Turn up to a dance class wearing
head to toe Lycra™
(extra point for male contenders).

When auditioning for the choir perform a thrash metal song... badly.

Join the volleyball team. Call your teammates 'Champ' and 'Tiger' and encourage them to refer to you as 'Coach'. Initiate high fives at any opportune moment.

While playing football/netball, at a random point in the game run off the pitch screaming and waving your arms in the air.

Attend a meeting of the
literature appreciation society.
Compare and contrast the
characters of Spider-Man and
Batman. Claim Spider-Man is a
latter-day Hamlet and
Batman is Macbeth.

Go to an art class and recreate a life-size papier mâché model of yourself — naked.

5 point dares

Attend a dance class. Put on 'Axel Foley's Theme' and perform 'the robot'.

After training, kneel in front of the water fountain and exclaim, 'With God as my witness I will never go thirsty again.'

Audition for the orchestra…
on the kazoo.

At the end of a football/netball/
hockey match suggest that it
would be nice if you concluded
with a prayer.

Become a member of the amateur dramatics society. Cultivate a new accent that you can phase in as your own, i.e. German, Scottish, Transylvanian. As soon as you leave the stage revert to your own accent.

During athletics training, keep
on running as fast as you can for
as long as you can. Throw up
if you need to.

10 point dares

Turn up at gymnastics club with the front of your shorts wet. Tell onlookers that you get *really* excited when tumbling.

Arrive at the swimming pool wearing your trunks backwards. Belly flop off the high board and doggy paddle into other swimmers' lanes. Ask if you have made the team.

When at athletics training, squat in the sandpit and pretend to take a number two.

Captain the ultimate frisbee team. For a whole semester. Go on. Even wear the T-shirt.

Scores

There were a total of 95 points up for grabs in this section.

If you scored 0–30 points: Come on, deadbeat, why are you wasting your time?

If you scored 31–60 points: Great work. Well done!

If you scored 61+ points: Wow! Go to the top of the class.

The Grand Total

There were a total of 425 points to be awarded in this book.

If you scored 0–150 points: You're a loser – simple as that. You deserve every moment of educational boredom coming to you.

If you scored 151–300 points: Well you certainly tried, didn't you? You deserve a medal for all the stupid things you have done and for all the confusion you have inflicted upon your fellow students.

If you scored 300+ points: You are the ultimate daredevil, on a par with Evil Knievel.

ALSO AVAILABLE

When stealing someone's stapler just isn't funny any more, beat office tedium with these dares that are guaranteed to perplex your manager:

- After every sentence, say 'mon' in a bad Jamaican accent.
- Vacuum around your desk — for half an hour.
- Attach a sign that says FAX to the paper shredder.

The office will never be the same.

Play the game, if you dare…

Summersdale Publishers Ltd * £2.99 * ISBN 1 84024 453 4

www.summersdale.com